## "BRING THE CLASSICS TO LIFE"

# The Man in the Iron Mask

## LEVEL 3

*Series Designer*
Philip J. Solimene

*Editor*
Laura M. Toles

**EDCON**
Long Island, New York

*Story Adapter*
**Robin M. Aiona**
*Author*
**Alexandre Dumas**

*About the Author*

Alexandre Dumas was the son of a general in Napoleon's army. His mother was a black woman who came from Santo Domingo. He wrote hundreds of books, so many in fact, that he had other writers assist him with his writing. The most famous of his works was *The Three Musketeers* followed by *The Count of Monte Cristo*. Alexandre earned a huge fortune in his day, but he lived carelessly. He died a poor man.


30 Montauk Blvd, Oakdale NY 11769
info@edconpublishing.com
1-888-553-3266

Visit our Web site at: www.edconpublishing.com

Printed in U.S.A.
ISBN# 1-55576-090-2

# CONTENTS

# WORDS USED

| Story 41 | Story 42 | Story 43 | Story 44 | Story 45 |
|---|---|---|---|---|
| **KEY WORDS** | | | | |
| adventure | guard | also | center | captain |
| charge | interest | imagine | cheer | dare |
| free | nod | parent | complete | delicious |
| order | queen | prove | giant | dine |
| palace | shine | spend | having | plan |
| sir | spoke | truth | sigh | reason |
| **NECESSARY WORDS** | | | | |
| dessert | confession | fuss | cloth | meal |
| marry | die | travel | invite | plate |
| musketeer | joy | | none | spot |
| prison | | | servant | |
| prisoner | | | tailor | |
| sword | | | | |

# WORDS USED

| Story 46 | Story 47 | Story 48 | Story 49 | Story 50 |
|---|---|---|---|---|
| | | **KEY WORDS** | | |
| act | enter | during | beach | barrel |
| exactly | chest | fault | harbor | die |
| explain | hammer | iron | possible | receive |
| main | handle | moan | speak | understood |
| wake | heart | sense | toward | weak |
| whole | hour | worth | trust | won |
| | | **NECESSARY WORDS** | | |
| hid | beat/beating | horrible | agree | boulder |
| mask | island | | meanwhile | lit |
| sinking | softly | | meeting | forgive |
| upset | worst | | quit | fought |
| | yesterday | | sail | |
| | | | surround | |

CTR C-41

# A Very Strange Dinner

## *PREPARATION*

### *Key Words*

**adventure** (ad ven′ chər) a fun-filled or strange happening

*Our trip to the police station was a great adventure.*

**charge** (chärj) to be left with the care of someone or something

*Emma was in charge of her brother while her mother was busy.*

**free** (frē) not held back or locked up

*Charles pulled free from his grandmother's hand.*

**order** (ôr′ dər) something that tells you what you have to do

*Billy had an order to come home right after school.*

**palace** (pal′ is) the home of a king and his wife or someone else important

*We saw the king standing outside of the palace.*

**sir** (sėr) a polite name to call someone

*Kerry always remembered to call the policeman sir.*

# A Very Strange Dinner

### *Necessary Words*

**dessert** (di zert´) pie, cake, ice cream, fruit or something else served at the end of a meal

*I love to eat cake for dessert.*

**marry** (mar´ ē) join as man and wife

*Jenny will marry the man she loves.*

**musketeer** (mus´ kə tir´) a man who watched over and made sure no one hurt the King of France; a soldier that carried a musket

*The king never left the palace without a musketeer by his side.*

**prison** (priz´ n) a building where people are locked up for breaking the law

*The robber was sent to prison for ten years.*

**prisoner** (priz´ nər) someone who is locked up in a prison

*The prisoner was very sorry for what he did.*

**sword** (sôrd) a very long, pointed knife used in fighting

*You must be very careful with a sword.*

### *People*

**D'Artagnan** is the head of the musketeers.

**Athos** was once a musketeer with his friend D'Artagnan.

**King Louis XIV** was the King of France from 1643-1715.

**Aramis** is a leader in the church of France. He was once a musketeer with his friends Athos and D'Artagnan.

**Baisemeaux** is the man in charge of the Bastille.

### *Places*

**France** is a country in Europe.

**Bastille** is an old building in France used as a prison.

CTR C-41

# A Very Strange Dinner

*The king took D'Artagnan's sword and threw it to the ground!*

| **Preview:** | 1. Read the name of the story.<br>2. Look at the picture.<br>3. Read the sentence under the picture.<br>4. Read the first paragraph of the story.<br>5. Then answer the following question. |
|---|---|

You learned from your preview that the king was

___ a. a happy man.
___ b. going to prison.
___ c. married.
___ d. not married.

*Turn to the Comprehension Check on page 10 for the right answer.*

***Now read the story.***

Read to find out how D'Artagnan fools the king.

# A Very Strange Dinner

D'Artagnan and Athos were driving through the gates of the Bastille in a coach. D'Artagnan did not want to take his friend to prison. He knew that he must, since the king told him to. King Louis XIV was angry. Athos's son loved the same girl as the king. Athos asked the king if his son could marry the girl. The king got very angry. He signed an order for D'Artagnan to take Athos to prison.

The two friends reached the last gate. D'Artagnan cried, "Look there, Athos!"

It was their old friend Aramis. Both men thought about the many adventures they had all had. Twenty years ago, Aramis, Athos and their friend Porthos were musketeers. Now, only D'Artagnan was a musketeer.

Athos was sad. He did not want Aramis to know he was going to prison.

D'Artagnan said, "Don't worry, I have an idea."

Athos and D'Artagnan followed Aramis into the Bastille. They saw he was about to have dinner with the man in charge. His name was Baisemeaux.

"Hello," said D'Artagnan.

Baisemeaux jumped to his feet. "Hello, sir," he said. "What can I do for you?"

D'Artagnan appeared to be surprised. "You told me to come for dinner," replied D'Artagnan. "I would like my friend Athos to join us."

"Oh, my," said Baisemeaux. "I don't remember asking you to come."

"Well, then, we shall leave here at once! Come Athos," said D'Artagnan.

"No, no. Please stay and eat with us." Baisemeaux didn't want to hurt D'Artagnan's feelings. He knew that D'Artagnan was the king's head musketeer.

"I'm sorry. I can't stay," replied D'Artagnan, "but my friend Athos will be happy to join you. I shall return in time for dessert. I must see the king at once!"

Athos then sat down to join Aramis and Baisemeaux. D'Artagnan turned and ran from the room.

D'Artagnan rushed back to the palace. He knew Athos must feel strange. To think that Athos was supposed to be locked up in the Bastille — but no, he was eating dinner with the man in charge!

When D'Artagnan got to the palace, he ran straight to the king's room.

"Did you do it?" the king asked.

"Yes, Athos is in the Bastille," replied D'Artagnan.

"Well," said the king, "did he try to get away?"

"Oh, no, sir. I told him to run away but he would not. I even told him I would get him a horse to get away with but still he would not go. He said, 'Take me to prison as the king ordered.'"

"What!" screamed the king. "You did not listen to my orders?"

"I tried not to, sir. Maybe you should send me to prison, too," said D'Artagnan, quietly.

The king couldn't believe his ears. He said, "If I sign an order to put you in prison . . . it's for life!"

"I know," said D'Artagnan. "If you don't, you will look like a fool for letting me talk to you this way. Here's my sword."

The king took the sword and threw it to the ground! He knew it was a terrible thing to put a musketeer in prison. D'Artagnan grabbed the sword and put it to his neck, ready to kill himself.

The king ran to him and pushed the sword away. "Please D'Artagnan, don't do it. I'll write an order to set your friend Athos free."

D'Artagnan returned to the Bastille with the order in hand. He turned to Baisemeaux and said, "Sir, you have been eating with a prisoner of the king. I have an order here to set him free."

Baisemeaux turned white. "What's going on here?" he asked.

"Here is the order to set Athos free," replied D'Artagnan.

Baisemeaux didn't know what was going on. "Fine, take him away," he said. "This dinner has been a strange adventure."

Athos couldn't stop smiling. He was free. He thanked his friend and wondered how he did it.

"Let's go, Athos. I'll take you home now."

Once again, the two friends went through the gates of the prison. Only this time, Athos was free.

# A Very Strange Dinner

## COMPREHENSION CHECK

**Preview Answer:**

d. not married.

***Choose the best answer.***

1. D'Artagnan
   ___a. lived in the forest.
   ___b. worked at the Bastille.
   ___c. was the king's head musketeer.
   ___d. enjoyed his life on the farm.

2. At one time, D'Artagnan, Porthos, Aramis, and Athos were all
   ___a. kings.
   ___b. musketeers.
   ___c. enemies.
   ___d. in jail.

3. King Louis XIV sent Athos to prison because
   ___a. Athos's son stole money from the king.
   ___b. Athos was no longer a good musketeer.
   ___c. Athos's son loved the same woman as the king.
   ___d. Athos was a very dangerous person in France.

4. Baisemeaux was
   ___a. away from his job at the Bastille.
   ___b. in jail for a crime.
   ___c. a brother to the king.
   ___d. in charge of the Bastille.

5. When D'Artagnan and Athos arrived at the Bastille,
   ___a. Athos was locked up in a dark room.
   ___b. Baisemeaux knew that D'Artagnan was not telling the truth.
   ___c. D'Artagnan tricked Baisemeaux easily.
   ___d. Aramis did not remember who Athos was after such a long time.

6. D'Artagnan made arrangements for Athos to have dinner with Baisemeaux and Aramis because
   ___a. he knew that Athos was a good friend of Baisemeaux's.
   ___b. he thought the king would like Athos to have an enjoyable evening.
   ___c. he had somewhere to go and didn't want Aramis to be alone.
   ___d. he didn't want Aramis to know that Athos was being sent to prison.

7. D'Artagnan was
   ___a. a brave and clever man.
   ___b. a lazy, but proud man.
   ___c. a mean and angry man.
   ___d. a very frightened man.

8. The king set Athos free
   ___a. because he knew he had been wrong to send Athos to prison.
   ___b. because he cared for D'Artagnan and his wishes.
   ___c. because he wanted Athos to gather information for him.
   ___d. to take Baisemeaux's place at the Bastille.

9. Another name for this story could be
   ___a. "Dinner With Friends."
   ___b. "The Trick and the Trade."
   ___c. "Life at the Castle."
   ___d. "Locked up in the Bastille."

10. This story is mainly about
   ___a. how Baisemeaux became a musketeer.
   ___b. how the king came to dinner at the Bastille.
   ___c. how D'Artagnan kept Athos out of prison.
   ___d. how friends enjoy having dinner together.

*Check your answers with the key on page 67.*

# A Very Strange Dinner

## VOCABULARY CHECK

| adventure | charge | free | order | palace | sir |
|---|---|---|---|---|---|

### I. Sentences to Finish

***Fill in the blank in each sentence with the correct key word from the box above.***

1. The tigers at the zoo are not ________________ to wander.
2. The sailor always called the chief ________________ .
3. The guards stood on each side of the doors of the ________________ , waiting for the king.
4. Our day at the park was a real ________________ .
5. The baby-sitter was in ________________ of the three children.
6. The doctor left an ________________ that told how to care for the sick child.

### II. Word Search

***All the words in the box above are hidden in the puzzle below. They may be written from left to right or up and down. As you find each word, put a circle around it. One word, that is not a key word, has been done for you.***

```
H E T (O N E) M V U
P I H S R M W O D
A D V E N T U R E
L G I T S F U D B
A X J O N R M E V
C H A R G E L R S
E Z K O B E S I R
B P A L A C E T K
```

*Check your answers with the key on page 69.*

# The Secret Prisoner

## PREPARATION

### Key Words

| | | |
|---|---|---|
| **guard** | (gärd) | someone who watches someone or something carefully<br>*The guard stood outside the bank all day.* |
| **interest** | (in′ tər ist) | a feeling of wanting to know about something<br>*Kelly had an interest in basketball.* |
| **nod** | (nod) | to move the head up and down to say hello or yes<br>*I will nod when I see you.* |
| **queen** | (kwēn) | the wife of a king<br>*Anne was the Queen of France.* |
| **shine** | (shīn) | to be bright with light<br>*The sun will shine all day.* |
| **spoke** | (spōk) | to have said something<br>*Bill spoke to your mother two days ago.* |

# The Secret Prisoner

## *Necessary Words*

**confession** (kən fesh´ ən) an owning up to of your wrong doings

*Beth made a confession to the teacher about breaking the chair.*

**die** (dī) to stop living

*The plant will die if I don't water it.*

**joy** (joi) a strong feeling of being happy

*Ken was full of joy when he got an A on his homework.*

## *People*

**King Louis XIII** is the father of the twins.

**Philippe** is the secret prisoner that Aramis has come to talk to.

# The Secret Prisoner

*Aramis hands Philippe a small mirror and tells him to take a look at himself.*

**Preview:**

1. Read the name of the story.
2. Look at the picture.
3. Read the sentence under the picture.
4. Read the first two paragraphs of the story.
5. Then answer the following question.

You learned from your preview that the prison guard brought Aramis to

___ a. a brightly lit room.
___ b. a very dark room.
___ c. a very cold room.
___ d. an empty room.

*Turn to the Comprehension Check on page 16 for the right answer.*

***Now read the story.***

Read to find out what Philippe learns about himself.

# *The Secret Prisoner*

When Aramis and Baisemeaux finished eating, Aramis stood up. "It's now time to do what I came here for," he said.

Baisemeaux called to a guard. Aramis followed the guard down a dark hall. After he had walked a long way, the guard stopped and opened a big door. Aramis slowly walked inside and closed the door. He did not say a word until he heard the guard's footsteps go down the hall. It was very dark in the room. The only light came from a small window that let the moon shine through. Aramis looked around the room. He saw a young man sitting on a bed.

Aramis finally spoke, "Good-evening, Philippe."

The man on the bed didn't show interest in Aramis. He just gave a nod of his head.

"I have been told that you wish to make a confession," said Aramis. "I'm here to listen to it."

The man looked at Aramis and said, "I have done nothing wrong."

"Why then, are you in prison?" asked Aramis.

"I cannot answer that, sir," replied the man.

"Don't you have any idea at all?" Aramis asked.

"No," said the man.

"Well then," began Aramis, "listen to my story."

"Some years ago, the last King of France, Louis XIII, was very worried. He was so sad because he didn't have a son. He wondered who would be the King of France if he were to die. At last, the queen said she was going to have a baby. To the king's great joy, she had a baby boy. A few minutes later, someone came to get the king. What he saw made him sad. The queen was holding twin boys. This was not something to be happy about. He knew there could be only one new king. He knew that when the boys got older, they would fight about who would be king. The king knew that something had to be done right away. The king spoke to the queen. They decided to send one boy away. Very few people knew about the two babies. They sent the one boy away that very day. He would grow up in the countryside of France. He was never told who he really was. The other twin grew up to be the King of France. In time, he was told about his twin brother. To this day, the king wants nothing to do with his brother."

Aramis looked at the young man closely. "Philippe, do you know who the boy that went to the country *is*?"

"No, I do not think so, sir," said Philippe. He was starting to show some interest.

Aramis then took some money out of his pocket. On the money was a picture of the king. Philippe looked at it. He then gave it back to Aramis. He was getting excited.

"Have you never looked in a mirror?" Aramis asked.

"I'm sorry, but I do not know what a mirror is," answered Philippe.

"Here . . . " Aramis gave him a small mirror . . . "LOOK!"

Philippe spoke in a shaky voice, "No, it can't be." Aramis's eyes were shining and he kept nodding his head.

"Yes, yes Philippe, you were that baby. You should be the King of France."

# The Secret Prisoner

## COMPREHENSION CHECK

**Preview Answer:**

b. a very dark room.

***Choose the best answer.***

1. King Louis XIII and the queen
   ___a. did not have any children.
   ___b. had twin sons.
   ___c. had twin daughters.
   ___d. did not have any sons.

2. When Louis and Philippe were babies,
   ___a. Louis was sent away to the country.
   ___b. Philippe was very sick.
   ___c. Louis liked to play with Philippe.
   ___d. Philippe was sent away to the country.

3. Aramis
   ___a. was no help to Philippe at all.
   ___b. wanted to keep King Louis XIV's secret.
   ___c. went to the Bastille to help Philippe.
   ___d. told Baisemeaux about his plan.

4. Philippe was really
   ___a. a terrible man.
   ___b. a neighbor of King Louis XIV.
   ___c. the brother of Aramis.
   ___d. the twin brother of King Louis XIV.

(5.) The picture on the money did not mean anything to Philippe because
   ___a. he had never seen money before.
   ___b. he did not know what he, himself, looked like.
   ___c. he could not see anything in the dark room.
   ___d. he had no way to spend the money.

(6.) When Aramis gave Philippe the mirror,
   ___a. Philippe asked Aramis to please leave him alone.
   ___b. Philippe called Baisemeaux to take him out of the prison.
   ___c. Philippe began to understand the story that Aramis shared with him.
   ___d. Philippe did not care about what he saw in it.

7. King Louis XIV
   ___a. did not want anything to do with his brother.
   ___b. was sorry about what his parents had done.
   ___c. wanted to share everything with his brother.
   ___d. said he would give up everything for his brother.

8. Aramis believed that
   ___a. Louis should be the King of France.
   ___b. the story should be kept a secret forever.
   ___c. Philippe should be the King of France.
   ___d. the people of France should be told the secret.

△9. Another name for this story could be
   ___a. "Baisemeaux at Dinner."
   ___b. "Athos Visits Philippe."
   ___c. "Baisemeaux Closes the Bastille."
   ___d. "Athos in the Country."

[10.] This story is mainly about
   ___a. how Athos tricked Baisemeaux again.
   ___b. the large jail called the Bastille.
   ___c. the true story of Louis and Philippe.
   ___d. how Philippe learned about a mirror.

*Check your answers with the key on page 67.*

# The Secret Prisoner

## VOCABULARY CHECK

| guard | interest | nod | queen | shine | spoke |
|---|---|---|---|---|---|

### I. Sentences to Finish

***Fill in the blank in each sentence with the correct key word from the box above.***

1. When John asked if he could have another piece of cake, his mom gave a __________________ and smiled.

2. The king and __________________ had two sons.

3. My dad washed the car so it would __________________ .

4. Because I have an __________________ in school, my grades are good.

5. I __________________ to my dad about borrowing his car Saturday night.

6. The __________________ took the jewels out of the store and put them into the special truck.

### II. Making Sense of Sentences

***Are the following sentences true or false? Place an X next to the correct answer.***

1. If you have an <u>interest</u> in something, you want to know more about it. _____ True _____ False

2. The <u>queen</u> is the wife of the king. _____ True _____ False

3. If you <u>nod</u>, you move your head back and forth. _____ True _____ False

4. A <u>guard</u> watches someone or something carefully. _____ True _____ False

5. When something has a <u>shine</u>, it is very dark. _____ True _____ False

6. If you <u>spoke</u>, you said something. _____ True _____ False

*Check your answers with the key on page 69.*

# Philippe Tells His Story

## PREPARATION

### Key Words

**also** (ôl´ sō) besides; too
*My horse is very big and he is fast, also.*

**imagine** (i maj´ ən) to picture in one's head; to get an idea of
*I cannot imagine what you mean.*

**parent** (par´ ənt) a father or mother
*My teacher said to give the letter to a parent.*

**prove** (prüv) to show that something is true or right
*I will prove to you that I can win the race.*

**spend** (spend) to pass time
*Cathy may spend all day at the zoo.*

**truth** (trüth) that which is true
*You must always tell the truth.*

# Philippe Tells His Story

***Necessary Words***

| | | |
|---|---|---|
| **fuss** | (fus) | useless talk and worry about small things<br>*The baby made a fuss about the toy he dropped.* |
| **travel** | (trav´ əl) | to go from one place to another<br>*I like to travel by boat.* |

# Philippe Tells His Story

*Aramis listens to Philippe's story.*

***Preview:***

1. Read the name of the story.
2. Look at the picture.
3. Read the sentence under the picture.
4. Read the first three paragraphs of the story.
5. Then answer the following question.

You learned from your preview that Philippe had been a prisoner

___ a. since he was born.
___ b. since he was eighteen.
___ c. for eight years.
___ d. for eighteen years.

*Turn to the Comprehension Check on page 22 for the right answer.*

***Now read the story.***

Read to find out why Philippe was put in prison.

# Philippe Tells His Story

For a long time Philippe didn't move. All his life he thought he was a simple farm boy, not a king. He didn't know if Aramis spoke the truth. Then, just as if Aramis could read his thoughts, he gave Philippe some papers.

"These will prove to you that you are of high birth," said Aramis.

Philippe looked at the papers, then he spoke. "Thank you, sir. I've been in the Bastille for eight years. Many times I've wondered why. I have also wondered what happened to my teacher and his wife. I knew they were not my real parents, yet they made me feel like I was their son. Do you know what happened to them?"

"I only know they were killed eight years ago," answered Aramis.

"I think I now understand why," said Philippe. "Would you like to hear my story?"

"Yes, please tell me what happened," answered Aramis.

Philippe began his story.

"We lived a simple life in the country. My parents would spend their days teaching me how to work the farm. To tell you the truth, sometimes I thought it was strange that we never had visitors.

"One day I heard my teacher call for his wife. He told her that the letter from the queen fell in the well. He wanted to go down and get it. His wife cried. She said they could be killed for losing that letter. My teacher said they would get someone in town to go down in the well to get it. He said they would find someone who couldn't read.

"One night, when they thought I was sleeping, they left the farm quickly. I couldn't imagine that my parents knew the queen. I decided to go down in the well and see what was in the letter. After reading the letter, I knew that my parents were important people. The queen also asked about me in the letter. Do you understand how hard it was for me to believe that the queen knew me?"

Aramis nodded his head and said, "I imagine it must have been hard."

"It was," said Philippe. "And it was so hard not knowing why I was taken from the farm by two men. I was put in the back of a coach. A covering was placed over my eyes. I couldn't tell where we were going. I know that we travelled more than two days. All of this happened just one week after my teacher found the pieces of the wet letter under my bed. That night I heard him tell his wife that they had to tell the queen the truth. I could not imagine what the big fuss was about. The letter didn't say much at all. At the end of that week, the men came for me. I couldn't even say good-by to my parents. The next thing I knew, I was put in this room. I've been here for eight years with no visitors. When I found the note in my dinner tonight, I was surprised."

Aramis smiled, "I gave the guard money to put the note in your dinner."

"I decided to listen to the note and tell the guard that I wanted to make a confession," replied Philippe.

"I'm glad you did," said Aramis. He shook Philippe's hand.

"If you listen to me and do as I say," said Aramis, "you will be King of France. I must leave here now, but I'll be back soon. The next time you see me will be the last night you spend in prison. One day you will rule all of France as you should have been doing all these years. I will prove it to you."

"I have been a prisoner for many years. Even if I never see you again, I thank you for all you have told me about myself," said Philippe.

As Aramis stood up to leave he said, "Have no fear, I'll be back. You will soon be the King of France."

# Philippe Tells His Story

## COMPREHENSION CHECK

**Preview Answer:**

c. for eight years.

***Choose the best answer.***

1. At first, Philippe
   ___a. believed Aramis was sent to trick him.
   ___b. knew that Aramis wasn't telling the truth.
   ___c. was not sure if the story Aramis was telling was true.
   ___d. told Aramis to leave the dark room and never return.

2. To prove that his story was true,
   ___a. Aramis showed Philippe some special papers.
   ___b. Aramis brought Philippe back to the country.
   ___c. Aramis called in the king to tell the true story.
   ___d. Aramis took Philippe to meet the king.

3. The letter that fell into the well
   ___a. was from the King of France to Philippe.
   ___b. was from Aramis to Philippe's parents.
   ___c. was from Philippe to his parents.
   ___d. was from the Queen of France to Philippe's parents.

4. It was important that whatever was written in the letter
   ___a. be told to everyone in town.
   ___b. be kept a secret.
   ___c. be told to Philippe.
   ___d. be kept in a well.

5. Philippe's parents in the country were killed and Philippe was put in prison
   ___a. because they were planning to remove the king.
   ___b. so the people in the town could use the well.
   ___c. because the queen had written them a letter by mistake.
   ___d. so no one would ever learn that the king had twin sons.

6. First, Aramis paid a guard to put a note in Philippe's dinner. Then, Philippe found the note on his tray. Next,
   ___a. Aramis left the Bastille and never came back.
   ___b. Philippe told the guard he wanted to make a confession.
   ___c. Baisemeaux was called to Philippe's dark room.
   ___d. Philippe told the guard about the note he had found.

7. Aramis
   ___a. believed that Philippe would make a better king than Louis.
   ___b. did not know what to do about the secret.
   ___c. wanted Philippe to stay in the Bastille forever.
   ___d. decided to move Philippe to a safe place away from France.

8. Philippe was
   ___a. angry that Aramis had come to his room.
   ___b. only thinking about leaving the prison.
   ___c. glad he finally learned about himself.
   ___d. still not able to understand the story Aramis told him.

9. Another name for this story could be
   ___a. "Aramis fights for the king."
   ___b. "The French Countryside."
   ___c. "The Queen and her Sons."
   ___d. "An Answer to Philippe's Questions."

10. This story is mainly about
   ___a. how Aramis tricked the guards at the Bastille.
   ___b. how Baisemeaux took care of the Bastille.
   ___c. how Aramis and Philippe told each other all that they knew.
   ___d. how Philippe planned to leave his dark room at the Bastille.

*Check your answers with the key on page 67.*

# *Philippe Tells His Story*

## *VOCABULARY CHECK*

| also | imagine | parent | prove | spend | truth |
|---|---|---|---|---|---|

### *I. Sentences to Finish*

***Fill in the blank in each sentence with the correct key word from the box above.***

1. I like to __________________ an afternoon looking through books at the library.
2. John practiced the piano every day to __________________ to his teacher that he could play well.
3. I like to __________________ that, one day, I will be a very rich person.
4. It is important to tell the __________________ so that people will believe what you say.
5. I enjoy playing baseball, but I __________________ like to play basketball.
6. When a __________________ comes to school, it is fun to show your best work.

### *II. Crossword Puzzle*

***Fill in the puzzle with the key words from the box above. Use the meanings below to help you choose the right word.***

**Across**

1. to picture in one's head
3. to show that something is true
5. that which is true

**Down**

2. besides
3. a father or mother
4. to pass time

1. 2 3 4 5.

*Check your answers with the key on page 69.*

# A Visit to the King's Tailor

## PREPARATION

### Key Words

| | | |
|---|---|---|
| **center** | (sen´ tər) | the middle point, place or part<br>*The pitcher stands in the center of the field.* |
| **cheer** | (chir) | a feeling of happiness or joy<br>*We tried to get him to cheer up.* |
| **complete** | (kəm plēt´) | get done; finish<br>*I must complete my homework before I can play.* |
| **giant** | (ji´ ənt) | someone or something that is very large<br>*The giant dog jumped all over me.* |
| **having** | (hav´ ng) | 1. causing; making<br>*I am having her take the test now.*<br>2. carry on something; holding<br>*We are having a talk.* |
| **sigh** | (sī) | to let out air from the mouth and make a sound to show sadness or some other feeling<br>*I gave a sigh when I lost my ring again.* |

# A Visit to the King's Tailor

### *Necessary Words*

**cloth** (klôth) what most clothes are made of

*Nancy bought red cloth to make a new dress.*

**invite** (in vīt´) ask (someone) politely to come to someplace or do something with you

*I will invite all my friends to the party.*

**none** (nun) not any

*We have none of that candy left.*

**servant** (sėr´ vənt) someone who works in someone else's home

*There are five servants that work in that big house.*

**tailor** (tā´ lər) someone who makes clothes

*Dad likes to have all his clothes made by the same tailor.*

### *People*

**Mr. Fouquet** is the man in charge of all the money in France.

**Mr. Percerin** is the tailor who makes clothes for the king and other important people.

**Porthos** was once a musketeer with Aramis, D'Artagnan and Athos. He is now a very well-off man.

CTR C-44

# A Visit to the King's Tailor

*"None of these clothes fit me," said Porthos to his friend D'Artagnan.*

***Preview:***

1. Read the name of the story.
2. Look at the picture.
3. Read the sentence under the picture.
4. Read the first five paragraphs of the story.
5. Then answer the following question.

You learned from your preview that Porthos

___ a. was not happy to see D'Artagnan.
___ b. seemed to cheer up when D'Artagnan came to visit.
___ c. did not want to go to the king's party.
___ d. was giving a party for the king.

*Turn to the Comprehension Check on page 28 for the right answer.*

***Now read the story.***

Read to find out why Porthos has nothing to wear to the king's party.

# A Visit to the King's Tailor

The day after his strange dinner at the Bastille, D'Artagnan visited the home of a man who used to be a musketeer with him. He stood by the door and saw his dear friend Porthos sitting on a chair in the center of the room. There was clothing everywhere. Porthos had his head down. He looked sad.

D'Artagnan spoke up, "What's wrong my friend?"

Porthos looked up. He seemed to cheer up. "I'm so happy to see you," said Porthos.

"You didn't look very happy when I walked in the room," replied D'Artagnan.

Porthos gave a loud sigh. "I'm worried because I'm invited to a party for the king this weekend."

"You mean the party Mr. Fouquet is having for the king?" asked D'Artagnan.

"Yes, I've nothing to wear," replied Porthos.

D'Artagnan began laughing. "How can you say that? There are enough clothes in this room to last a year!"

Porthos didn't smile. "None of these clothes fit me."

"What? Why not?" D'Artagnan looked closely at his friend. Porthos had always been a giant of a man but he didn't look any bigger than the last time he had seen him.

"Do you remember my servant?" asked Porthos.

"Yes, what does he have to do with your clothes?" asked D'Artagnan.

"I decided it was too much trouble to go to the tailor every time I needed new clothes. I came up with the idea of having someone go in my place," said Porthos.

"Good idea. It's too bad you picked your servant. He's such a small man — and you're so big," replied D'Artagnan.

"Oh, no," said Porthos. "I knew that, so I had him eat more. When he was as big as me, I had him go to the tailor once a week and get me new clothes. Things were going along fine. Then I was called away and had to leave home for a while. I told my servant to keep going to the tailor once a week. I've just returned, and I see that he did go to the tailor. I've all these clothes to prove it! I made only one mistake. I forgot to tell my servant to stop getting bigger. All these clothes are much too big for me. My servant is now a giant with many new clothes. On the other hand, *I* have to go to the party for the king with only my old clothes to wear."

D'Artagnan tried not to laugh, but he couldn't help it. "Cheer up my friend. I'll take you to Mr. Percerin right now," said D'Artagnan.

Porthos sighed again, "I don't think that even the king's tailor could complete clothes for me in time for the party."

"Don't worry," said D'Artagnan. "He will do it for me. I know him well."

When the two friends got to Mr. Percerin's place, they found him in the center of the shop. He told D'Artagnan that there was no way he could do it. He said he was much too busy working on the king's clothes. Just then, they heard someone come into the store. It was Aramis.

"Sir, I know that you can complete the clothes for my friend Porthos and for the king. Will you please do it for me?" asked Aramis.

"Yes sir, I'll do it for you. Please go to the back room and wait for me, sir," said the tailor to Porthos.

D'Artagnan sat down to wait. He wanted to find out why Aramis was there. He thought it was strange that he kept seeing Aramis everywhere. When he heard that Aramis wanted to see the king's new clothes, he couldn't believe it. He was even more surprised when Mr. Percerin gave Aramis a piece of the cloth from the king's new clothes. D'Artagnan knew that no one was supposed to see the clothes before the party.

When Aramis left, D'Artagnan was still sitting there. He was trying to understand what his good friend Aramis was up to. He decided he would just have to wait until the party to find out.

# A Visit to the King's Tailor

## COMPREHENSION CHECK

### *Choose the best answer.*

1. After his dinner at the Bastille, D'Artagnan
 ___a. visited his friend Aramis.
 ___b. visited the king.
 ___c. visited his friend Porthos.
 ___d. visited Philippe.

2. Mr. Fouquet
 ___a. was a tailor for the king.
 ___b. was locked up in the Bastille.
 ___c. was living in another country.
 ___d. was giving a party for the king.

3. Porthos's plan to send his servant to be fitted for his clothes
 ___a. did not please the tailor.
 ___b. didn't work out well because his servant gained too much weight.
 ___c. left the servant with no clothes to wear.
 ___d. did not please his servant.

4. Mr. Percerin
 ___a. made cakes.
 ___b. made horseshoes.
 ___c. made candles.
 ___d. made clothes.

5. While D'Artagnan and Porthos were at the tailor's place,
 ___a. Aramis came in.
 ___b. Athos came to have clothes made.
 ___c. the king picked up his clothes.
 ___d. the queen arrived.

**Preview Answer:**

b. seemed to cheer up when D'Artagnan came to visit.

6. Porthos got his new clothes because
 ___a. D'Artagnan spoke to the tailor.
 ___b. the tailor was not very busy this time of year.
 ___c. Aramis asked the tailor to take the time to make them.
 ___d. the tailor was afraid to say no to Porthos.

7. Aramis asked the tailor
 ___a. to see the new clothes he was making for the king.
 ___b. to make him the same clothes as Porthos wore.
 ___c. to find a servant to be fitted for the king's clothes.
 ___d. to order material for Aramis's new clothes.

8. D'Artagnan
 ___a. knew what Aramis was doing.
 ___b. expected to find Aramis at Mr. Percerin's store.
 ___c. didn't know about the king's party.
 ___d. believed that Aramis was planning something.

9. Another name for this story could be
 ___a. "D'Artagnan's Adventure."
 ___b. "New Clothes."
 ___c. "The Very Large Servant."
 ___d. "The Battle."

10. This story is mainly about
 ___a. Aramis helping Porthos get new clothes for the party.
 ___b. D'Artagnan's strange dinner at the Bastille.
 ___c. D'Artagnan's visit with his old friend Porthos.
 ___d. the grand party that would be given for the King of France and his friends.

*Check your answers with the key on page 67.*

# A Visit to the King's Tailor

## VOCABULARY CHECK

| center | cheer | complete | giant | having | sigh |
|---|---|---|---|---|---|

### I. Sentences to Finish

***Fill in the blank in each sentence with the correct key word from the box above.***

1. Paul drew a big circle in the ________________ of his paper.
2. The children worked hard to ________________ the costumes in time for the play.
3. We are ________________ a book fair at school next month.
4. Mary gave a ________________ when she had to take another test.
5. There was a ________________ in the story, "Jack and the Beanstalk."
6. When our team won the game, there was great ________________ and excitement.

### II. Matching

***Write the letter of the correct meaning from Column B next to the key word in Column A.***

| | Column A | | Column B |
|---|---|---|---|
| _____1. | center | a. | to let out air from the mouth and make a sound of sadness |
| _____2. | cheer | b. | someone or something that is very large |
| _____3. | complete | c. | the middle point, place or part |
| _____4. | giant | d. | a feeling of happiness |
| _____5. | having | e. | causing; holding |
| _____6. | sigh | f. | finish |

*Check your answers with the key on page 70.*

**CTR C-45**

# Another Dinner at the Bastille

## *PREPARATION*

### *Key Words*

| | | |
|---|---|---|
| **captain** | (kap´ tən) | a person in charge of a group<br>*He was the captain of the football team.* |
| **dare** | (der) | be brave enough; to have no fear<br>*You would not dare go alone!* |
| **delicious** | (di lish´ əs) | very good to eat or smell<br>*The bread smells delicious.* |
| **dine** | (dīn) | to eat dinner<br>*I dine at the same time every night.* |
| **plan** | (plan) | a way of making or doing something that has been worked out before<br>*We had a plan to go to the park after school.* |
| **reason** | (rē´ zn) | why something is done<br>*I have a good reason for wearing no shoes.* |

# Another Dinner at the Bastille

### *Necessary Words*

**meal** (mēl) breakfast, lunch or dinner
*I drink milk with every meal.*

**plate** (plāt) a round dish that is almost flat
*He ate all the food on his plate.*

**spot** (spot) a small mark on something
*There is a spot on my new dress.*

CTR C-45

# Another Dinner at the Bastille

*Baisemeaux picked up the order and looked at it. He couldn't believe his eyes!*

***Preview:***

1. Read the name of the story.
2. Look at the picture.
3. Read the sentences under the picture.
4. Read the first two paragraphs of the story.
5. Then answer the following question.

You learned from your preview that Aramis and D'Artagnan

___ a. never got along.
___ b. always dined together.
___ c. made plans to free Philippe.
___ d. were good friends.

*Turn to the Comprehension Check on page 34 for the right answer.*

***Now read the story.***

Read to find out how Aramis tricks Baisemeaux.

# Another Dinner at the Bastille

Once again Aramis was to dine at the Bastille. Baisemeaux said they were to have a delicious meal.

Aramis did not feel good. He was thinking about his plan. He was also worried about D'Artagnan. He knew his friend felt something was strange. D'Artagnan was the captain of the guards. If he knew of the plan, he would stop him. They might be good friends, but being true to the king was much more important.

Aramis tried to think about the delicious food on his plate. Just then, a prison guard walked into the room. Aramis got ready to begin his plan.

"How dare you come in here while we are eating!" roared Baisemeaux to the guard.

The guard replied, "I'm sorry, sir. It's an order from the king."

Baisemeaux told the guard to wait until after dinner. The guard was about to leave the room, but Aramis stopped him.

He said to Baisemeaux, "Please do what you must. I will wait. The guard said it was an order from the king."

Baisemeaux was afraid. He knew Aramis was a very important man in France. He did not want to get in trouble.

He called to the captain of the guards. "Bring the order here now."

Baisemeaux read the order and put it down. He said, "There is no reason to rush. This is only an order to let a prisoner go. This prisoner is not important."

Aramis said, "Let me see that paper." After he read it, he put it on the table. "Why do you say it's not important to let Philippe go? He has been in prison for many years. You should let him leave at once. This is an order from the king."

"What do you mean? This order is not to let the prisoner Philippe go. It is for another prisoner," said Baisemeaux.

Aramis said, "You are wrong. I also read the order. It said to let Philippe go."

Baisemeaux picked up the order and looked at it. He could not believe his eyes.

"This can't be. I know this order had another name on it. It didn't say Philippe. There was also a spot on the paper that is not here now," said Baisemeaux.

Aramis tried to stay calm. He did not dare let Baisemeaux know he was worried. He said, "Do you have a reason not to believe your own eyes?"

Baisemeaux didn't know what to do. He did not know that Aramis had changed the orders on the table. When Baisemeaux was eating, Aramis had put an order from his pocket on the table. He then put the real order in his pocket.

Baisemeaux said, "Maybe I had too much to drink tonight. I was sure I saw another name. I will let Philippe go tomorrow."

Aramis was getting worried. "Why don't you let him go tonight?" Aramis asked.

"Because tonight it is dark and cold. He will have no place to go. Tomorrow will be better for him," Baisemeaux replied.

"I will take him back to the church with me. He can stay there for the night," said Aramis.

Baisemeaux thought that the evening was very strange. It seemed that every time he dined with Aramis, something happened. He said, "If you wish, you may take him."

Aramis jumped from his chair. He did not even wait to finish eating. He told Baisemeaux to have the guard take him to Philippe. Baisemeaux called the guard back once again. He told him to take Aramis to Philippe and let him go.

Baisemeaux finished eating alone. He thought it would be a long time before he had Aramis over for dinner again.

# Another Dinner at the Bastille

## COMPREHENSION CHECK

**Preview Answer:**

d. were good friends.

***Choose the best answer.***

1. Aramis and Baisemeaux
   ___a. were on their way to the king's party.
   ___b. were having dinner together at the Bastille.
   ___c. were going to bring a prisoner to the Bastille.
   ___d. were leaving the Bastille for a trip to the city.

(2.) In the beginning of the story, Aramis thought that
   ___a. all would go well with his plan.
   ___b. he better not continue with his plan.
   ___c. D'Artagnan might spoil his plan.
   ___d. Baisemeaux knew about his plan.

3. While Baisemeaux was eating his dinner, Aramis
   ___a. switched the orders for the prisoner that was to be set free.
   ___b. secretly took Philippe out of the Bastille through a back door.
   ___c. asked the guard to call the king.
   ___d. brought D'Artagnan to the Bastille.

4. The order written on the paper without the spot said that
   ___a. Baisemeaux was to take D'Artagnan prisoner.
   ___b. Baisemeaux was to call D'Artagnan.
   ___c. Baisemeaux was to go to the party for the king.
   ___d. Baisemeaux was to set Philippe free.

5. Baisemeaux
   ___a. was sure Philippe was the right man to set free.
   ___b. questioned the fact that Philippe's name was really the name on the order.
   ___c. wanted Philippe and the guard to join him for dinner.
   ___d. decided that he didn't want to be in charge of the Bastille any longer.

6. Aramis asked Baisemeaux
   ___a. to wait for the morning to let Philippe out.
   ___b. to keep Philippe in the Bastille for a long time.
   ___c. to call the king and check on the order to free Philippe.
   ___d. to let him take Philippe back to his church that night.

7. Baisemeaux's dinners with Aramis
   ___a. were always quiet times for Baisemeaux.
   ___b. were something he would often do in the future.
   ___c. were becoming more and more strange.
   ___d. were full of fun and laughter.

8. At the end of the story,
   ___a. Aramis was on his way to take Philippe out of the Bastille.
   ___b. Baisemeaux had Aramis arrested for changing an order from the king.
   ___c. the guard told Baisemeaux what had really happened.
   ___d. the king was on his way to the Bastille to see Aramis.

△9. Another name for this story could be
   ___a. "Baisemeaux's Plan."
   ___b. "Fun with Aramis."
   ___c. "Philippe Returns to the Country."
   ___d. "Setting Philippe Free."

[10.] This story is mainly about
   ___a. what Philippe did when he left the Bastille.
   ___b. how Aramis tricked Baisemeaux into letting Philippe out of prison.
   ___c. why Baisemeaux did not want to take the order from the guard.
   ___d. how King Louis set Philippe free.

*Check your answers with the key on page 67.*

# Another Dinner at the Bastille

## VOCABULARY CHECK

| captain | dare | delicious | dine | plan | reason |
|---|---|---|---|---|---|

### I. Sentences to Finish

***Fill in the blank in each sentence with the correct key word from the box above.***

1. The chocolate ice cream sandwich was ________________ .
2. The ________________ that I couldn't visit my friend was that I had so much homework.
3. The ________________ of a ship gives the orders about how the ship will be run.
4. We worked in small groups to ________________ each part of the class book we were making.
5. Sometimes my parents ________________ after all of the children have finished their meal.
6. Would you ________________ to climb a mountain or jump from an airplane?

### II. Crossword Puzzle

***Fill in the puzzle with the key words from the box above. Use the meanings below to help you choose the right word.***

**Across**

1. very good to eat or smell
3. to eat dinner
5. a way of making or doing something that has been worked out before

**Down**

1. to be brave enough
2. why something is done
4. a person in charge of a group

1 2 3 4 5

*Check your answers with the key on page 70.*

**CTR C-46**

# The Switch

## *PREPARATION*

### *Key Words*

**act** (akt) to behave like
*Don't act like a clown.*

**exactly** (eg zakt′ lē) in the same way; just so
*She was wearing exactly the same dress as I had on.*

**explain** (ek splān′) to tell how to do something
*I will explain the game only once.*

**main** (mān) most important; largest
*We will go to the main door of the store.*

**wake** (wāk) stop sleeping; to awake
*I wake up early in the morning.*

**whole** (hōl) full; complete
*Please tell me the whole story.*

# The Switch

***Necessary Words***

| | | |
|---|---|---|
| **hid** | (hid) | to have covered up so that something couldn't be seen<br>*She hid her money under the bed.* |
| **mask** | (mask) | a covering to put on over the face and/or head<br>*She had a pretty mask on at the party.* |
| **sinking** | (singk´ ng) | going down; falling slowly<br>*The penny was sinking to the bottom of the pool very fast.* |
| **upset** | (up set´) | a feeling of being very worried; not calm<br>*We were very upset before the race.* |

# The Switch

*"It would be best if you forget that you are the king," said Aramis. "Soon you won't be giving any orders."*

***Preview:***

1. Read the name of the story.
2. Look at the picture.
3. Read the sentences under the picture.
4. Read the first five paragraphs of the story.
5. Then answer the following question.

You learned from your preview that, soon, Philippe would be

___ a. King of the Bastille.
___ b. King of France.
___ c. King of England.
___ d. King of the Guards.

*Turn to the Comprehension Check on page 40 for the right answer.*

***Now read the story.***

Read to find out how Aramis had King Louis XIV change places with Philippe.

# The Switch

Philippe didn't say a word when he saw Aramis. He did not know how to act. He didn't want to seem too happy in front of the guard.

Aramis said, "Come with me, Philippe. The king has set you free."

They followed the guard to the main door of the prison. Philippe followed Aramis to his coach. Aramis said, "Please get in my king."

Now that they were alone, Philippe began to talk. "I don't know how I can ever thank you, sir."

Aramis replied, "Please don't call me 'sir,' because tomorrow you will be the King of France."

As they rode along, Aramis began to explain his plan to Philippe. He told him that his brother, Louis, was at a party. Mr. Fouquet, who was in charge of all the money in France, was having the party. The party was to last for the whole weekend. Aramis told Philippe that he had clothes made to look exactly like Louis's clothes.

"How did you have that done?" asked Philippe.

"I told the king's tailor I wanted to have a painting done of the king. I said it would be a present for the king. I then explained that I wanted the painting to show the king in his new clothes. The tailor couldn't say no. I then had my own tailor make some clothes to look exactly like the ones in the painting," replied Aramis.

On the way to the party, Aramis went over everything that Philippe should know. Philippe had read over the papers that Aramis gave to him on his last visit to the Bastille. Philippe remembered everything. There was no reason for him to worry; he looked exactly like his brother. He even sounded like him.

When they got to the party, Philippe was told to hide until someone came to get him.

After a while the king went to his room for the night. He was very upset. He was angry at Mr. Fouquet. He thought Mr. Fouquet had a better palace than his, with more servants, too!

As the king started to fall asleep, the strangest thing happened. It seemed to the king that his bed was sinking into the ground. The king opened his eyes and saw three men looking down at him in his bed. He called for help. When no one came to help him, the king thought he was still asleep. He tried to wake up. He looked around and saw he was no longer in his room.

"Where am I and who are you? I am the King of France! I order you to leave me at once!" screamed the king.

Aramis wore a mask so that the king could not see him. He said, "You are in a secret room underground. I had this room built to sneak you out of this castle. And it would be best if you forget that you are the king. Soon you won't be giving any orders."

While the king was heading to the Bastille, Philippe was now in his brother's bed. He was trying to decide how he would act tomorrow.

Once again Aramis was at the main gate of the Bastille. He ordered a guard to wake Baisemeaux.

Aramis took the mask off his face. He waited for Baisemeaux.

Baisemeaux came to the gate in his night clothes. He asked Aramis what was going on.

Aramis replied, "Last night you let the wrong prisoner go. It was supposed to be Philippe. The whole thing was a mistake."

"What do you mean?" asked Baisemeaux. He looked like he was not awake yet.

"If the king finds out you let the wrong prisoner out, you could be in a lot of trouble," replied Aramis. "But don't worry, I have returned the prisoner to you. He is in my coach. I'll get him for you."

"How can I ever thank you?" asked Baisemeaux.

"Just lock him up and let no one see him. He has gone mad. He thinks he is the king," replied Aramis.

Once the king was locked up, he began to scream, and he didn't plan to stop until he was out of the Bastille.

CTR C-46

# The Switch

## COMPREHENSION CHECK

**Preview Answer:**

b. King of France.

***Choose the best answer.***

(1.) In the coach on the way from the Bastille,
___a. Philippe was angry at Aramis for taking him out of the palace.
___b. Philippe was happy about Aramis's plan to make him King of France.
___c. Aramis didn't tell Philippe anything about his plans for the party.
___d. Aramis told Philippe he had changed his mind about making him King.

2. The tailor showed Aramis the king's clothes because
___a. he knew that Aramis wanted to get rid of King Louis.
___b. D'Artagnan said the king would not mind.
___c. Aramis told the tailor he needed to know exactly how the king would look for a painting.
___d. the tailor was very happy with the material and colors he had used to make such fine clothes.

(3.) King Louis was upset with Mr. Fouquet because
___a. Louis thought that Mr. Fouquet had more wealth than he did.
___b. Mr. Fouquet said some terrible things to the king about money.
___c. the party was not what the king thought it would be.
___d. a special friend of the king's had not been invited.

4. The man wearing the mask was
___a. D'Artagnan.
___b. Mr. Fouquet.
___c. Baisemeaux.
___d. Aramis.

(5.) When Aramis arrived at the Bastille,
___a. he asked Baisemeaux to put him under arrest.
___b. he took Louis out of prison.
___c. he tricked Baisemeaux again.
___d. he put the real Philippe back in jail.

6. How did Aramis explain Louis's screams that he was the King of France?
___a. Aramis said that Philippe was hoping to trick them into letting him go.
___b. Aramis told Baisemeaux that Philippe had lost his mind and imagined he was King.
___c. Aramis said that Philippe had forgotten his name.
___d. Aramis told Baisemeaux the truth about everything.

7. At the end of the story, Baisemeaux
___a. was thankful to Aramis.
___b. was angry at Aramis.
___c. was sad for Philippe.
___d. was angry at the king.

8. During Mr. Fouquet's party,
___a. Aramis made a big fuss in the middle of dinner.
___b. Baisemeaux came in to say that he had made a mistake.
___c. D'Artagnan became angry because Mr. Fouquet's palace was nicer than his.
___d. Aramis took King Louis out of his bed and put Philippe in his place.

△9. Another name for this story could be
___a. "Mr. Fouquet's Palace."
___b. "A New King for France."
___c. "King Louis Rules."
___d. "A Party at the Bastille."

[10.] This story is mainly about
___a. why King Louis was angry with Aramis.
___b. how the tailor made Philippe clothes to match King Louis's clothes.
___c. why Baisemeaux had trouble at the Bastille.
___d. how Aramis removed King Louis and put Philippe in his place.

*Check your answers with the key on page 67.*

# The Switch

## VOCABULARY CHECK

| act | exactly | explain | main | wake | whole |
|---|---|---|---|---|---|

### I. Sentences to Finish

***Fill in the blank in each sentence with the correct key word from the box above.***

1. Kim was able to eat the ________________ pie, so she won the pie-eating contest.
2. The children knew how they should ________________ during their class trip to the city.
3. The teacher asked Pedro to ________________ how he found the answer to the question.
4. When I ________________ in the morning, the first thing I do is look out the window to see what the weather is like.
5. My mom makes pizza ________________ the way I like it.
6. The ________________ room in our house is the living room.

### II. Mixed-up Words

***First, unscramble the letters in Column A to spell out the key words. Then, match the key words with the right meaning in Column B by drawing a line from the word to the meaning.***

| Column A | Column B |
|---|---|
| 1. ohwle ________________ | a. stop sleeping |
| 2. niam ________________ | b. to tell how to do something |
| 3. taclexy ________________ | c. to behave like |
| 4. ekwa ________________ | d. most important |
| 5. tca ________________ | e. in the same way |
| 6. lpeianx ________________ | f. full; complete |

*Check your answers with the key on page 70.*

**CTR C-47**

# *The Story is Told*

## *PREPARATION*

### *Key Words*

| | | |
|---|---|---|
| **enter** | (en´ tər) | go into; come into<br>*You enter a house through the door.* |
| **chest** | (chest) | the front part of you, above your tummy<br>*He covered his chest with a shirt.* |
| **hammer** | (ham´ ər) | to hit again and again<br>*I will hammer at the rock until it cracks.* |
| **handle** | (han´ dl) | to take care of<br>*The teacher will handle the money for the small children.* |
| **heart** | (härt) | the part of you that keeps you living<br>*He could hear his heart if he listened carefully.* |
| **hour** | (our) | one of twelve same parts of time between the middle of the day and the middle of the night<br>*I had one hour to finish my work.* |

# *The Story is Told*

### *Necessary Words*

**beat/beating** (bēt) to hit again and again
*We could hear the rain beat on the roof.*

**island** (ī´ lənd) a piece of land that has water on all sides of it
*Kevin ran around the island in one day.*

**softly** (sôft´ ly) not loudly
*Susan spoke very softly.*

**worst** (wėrst) not good at all; very bad
*This is the worst thing that could happen.*

**yesterday** (yes´ tər dē) the day before today
*I saw a black cat yesterday.*

### *Places*

**Belle-Isle** is an island that Mr. Fouquet gives to Aramis so that Aramis will have a place to hide from the king.

CTR C-47

# The Story is Told

*Aramis pounds on Porthos's door to wake him.
He will need his help if he is to get away safely.*

**Preview:**
1. Read the name of the story.
2. Look at the picture.
3. Read the sentences under the picture.
4. Read the first six paragraphs of the story.
5. Then answer the following question.

You learned from your preview that Aramis had left Philippe at Mr. Fouquet's palace

___ a. to teach him a lesson.
___ b. to give him some time to be alone.
___ c. to give him time to start acting like a king.
___ d. to bring his brother to the Bastille.

*Turn to the Comprehension Check on page 46 for the right answer.*

***Now read the story.***

Read to find out what Mr. Fouquet does when he learns what Aramis has done.

# *The Story is Told*

The next day when Philippe opened his eyes, he saw D'Artagnan enter his room.

"Good morning, sir," said D'Artagnan. "Can I do anything for you this morning?"

"Yes, I wish to see Aramis, now," spoke Philippe.

When Aramis entered the room, Philippe said to D'Artagnan, "We wish to talk alone. Please leave here now."

When the door closed, Philippe spoke. "When I woke this morning, I could hear my heart hammer in my chest. Why did you leave me alone at Mr. Fouquet's?"

"I'm sorry, sir. I had to take care of your brother. He is now safely locked up in the Bastille. Please don't worry. Everything is going along as planned," answered Aramis.

Just then, there was a knock at the door. It was Mr. Fouquet.

"I'll handle this, sir," said Aramis. "Don't worry."

Aramis told Mr. Fouquet that the king was resting now, but that he had a message from the king.

As the two men walked down the hall, Aramis told Fouquet that the king was having a wonderful time.

"Are you sure?" asked Fouquet. "I thought the king was angry with me."

"Oh, no, not this king," answered Aramis.

"What do you mean, 'not this king?'" asked Fouquet.

Aramis had decided that he must tell Mr. Fouquet about the two kings because he needed his help. You see, Fouquet was in charge of all the money in France. So, once again, Aramis found himself telling the story of the twin boys and how he had planned to switch them.

As Aramis got to the end of his story, he felt his heart beating faster. Mr. Fouquet had his hand on his chest and looked like he was about to fall.

"Do you know that you have done the worst thing that anyone in France could do? The king could have you killed for it!" said Fouquet with fire in his eyes.

Aramis knew that he must calm down if he was going to handle this the right way. He spoke very softy. "Mr. Fouquet, no one is going to be killed. No one but you and I know what has happened."

"Soon all of France will know because I must go and free the true king," replied Fouquet.

"Please listen to me," said Aramis. "You and I know that both brothers could be the true king. The king that knew you yesterday, *hates* you. The king that you will see today, *likes* you. Don't you want to have a king that likes you?"

"As soon as I set the king free, he'll love me," answered Fouquet. I'll give you four hours to get away from here. Once the king is free, he'll surely kill you. Go now!"

Aramis couldn't believe his ears. He wished he could make Fouquet understand that Philippe would be a good and fair king.

"Where could I go in four hours, Mr. Fouquet? Don't do this, it would be a mistake," cried Aramis.

"I'll give you Belle-Isle. It's an island that I own. You will be safe there. Now go!" shouted Fouquet.

As Mr. Fouquet ran to get his horse, Aramis turned and ran down the hall. Just as he was about to enter his friend Porthos's room, he saw D'Artagnan.

"Please dear friend, don't stop me now. I must wake Porthos and leave here at once," said Aramis.

D'Artagnan knew something was wrong. He didn't stop his old friend. He turned and walked away. He hoped that his good friends were not in too much trouble.

Aramis knew that Porthos would come with him. He would need his help if he hoped to get away. He began to hammer on Porthos's door to wake him. When his tired friend woke up, Aramis told him that they must leave at once.

As the two old friends rode away on their horses, D'Artagnan watched from the house. He knew that he would soon find out what was going on. He only hoped that it wasn't too bad, but he had the feeling that his good friends were in deep trouble.

# The Story is Told

## COMPREHENSION CHECK

### Choose the best answer.

**Preview Answer:**

d. to bring his brother to the Bastille.

1. When D'Artagnan entered the king's room in the morning,
   ___a. he took away Aramis and put him in the Bastille.
   ___b. he did not know that it was really Philippe instead of Louis.
   ___c. he wondered why the king wanted to see Aramis so early.
   ___d. he knew right away that the king was not Louis.

2. Philippe
   ___a. had no worries at all about being king.
   ___b. made some mistakes that showed he was not the real king.
   ___c. changed his mind and no longer wanted to be king.
   ___d. was still not sure of himself and needed help from Aramis.

3. When Aramis told Mr. Fouquet about how he had switched the kings,
   ___a. Mr. Fouquet offered to give him the money he needed.
   ___b. Mr. Fouquet called D'Artagnan for help.
   ___c. Mr. Fouquet became very angry and upset.
   ___d. Mr. Fouquet went to speak with Philippe right away.

4. Aramis believed that
   ___a. Philippe had as much right to be king as did Louis.
   ___b. Mr. Fouquet would not tell anyone what had happened.
   ___c. Philippe would not make a good king after all.
   ___d. Mr. Fouquet could never be of any help with money.

5. Mr. Fouquet
   ___a. immediately called D'Artagnan to arrest Aramis.
   ___b. liked the idea of having Philippe as king instead of Louis.
   ___c. wanted to run away with Aramis to another country.
   ___d. gave Aramis the island of Belle-Isle so he could escape safely.

6. Aramis tried to make Mr. Fouquet change his mind by telling him that
   ___a. all of the prisons in France would be closed.
   ___b. the new king, Philippe, liked him better than Louis did.
   ___c. all the money that King Louis had would be given to him.
   ___d. the old king, Louis, would never hurt him.

7. At the end of the story, Mr. Fouquet
   ___a. said that he would not tell anyone the secret.
   ___b. asked D'Artagnan to ride with him to the prison.
   ___c. was on his way to free the king from the Bastille.
   ___d. sent a man to see Baisemeaux about what had happened.

8. First, Aramis ran down the hall toward Porthos's room. Then, Aramis spoke to D'Artagnan. Next,
   ___a. D'Artagnan turned and walked away.
   ___b. Porthos would not go with D'Artagnan.
   ___c. D'Artagnan arrested Aramis and Porthos.
   ___d. Porthos left the palace without Aramis.

9. Another name for this story could be
   ___a. "D'Artagnan and the King."
   ___b. "A Change of Plans."
   ___c. "Long Live King Philippe."
   ___d. "A Wonderful Party."

10. This story is mainly about
   ___a. why everyone knows Philippe is not the real king.
   ___b. how D'Artagnan saves Aramis, Porthos and Philippe.
   ___c. how Aramis, Porthos and Philippe come to be in terrible danger.
   ___d. why Aramis must always ask for help from Mr. Fouquet at his palace.

*Check your answers with the key on page 67.*

# The Story is Told

## VOCABULARY CHECK

| enter | chest | hammer | handle | heart | hour |
|---|---|---|---|---|---|

### I. Sentences to Finish

***Fill in the blank in each sentence with the correct key word from the box above.***

1. We ________________ the school through the main gates in the front of the building.
2. My friend Carla said she would ________________ all the plans for the bake sale, if we would bake the cakes.
3. Jan's ________________ beat faster and faster as she came nearer to the finish line.
4. The man used weights to help make his arms and his ________________ stronger.
5. Our clock makes a soft, ringing sound every ________________ .
6. We will ________________ the poles into the ground to put up the tent.

### II. Word Search

***All the words in the box above are hidden in the puzzle below. They may be written from left to right or up and down. As you find each word, put a circle around it. One word, that is not a key word, has been done for you.***

| | | | | | | | |
|---|---|---|---|---|---|---|---|
| (O | L | D) | P | I | K | Z | V |
| C | I | H | A | M | M | E | R |
| H | N | A | B | S | O | N | E |
| E | Z | N | E | H | X | T | P |
| S | K | D | C | O | B | E | X |
| T | A | L | M | U | Y | R | I |
| O | H | E | A | R | T | B | U |
| M | K | O | L | C | V | E | W |

*Check your answers with the key on page 71.*

# Will the Real King Please Stand Up?

## PREPARATION

### Key Words

**during** (dủr′ ing) through the whole time of
*We played inside during the storm.*

**fault** (fôlt) something that is not as it should be; mistake
*It was her fault that we lost the game.*

**iron** (i′ ərn) a very hard metal
*The hammer head is made of iron.*

**moan** (mōn) a long, low sound of pain
*We heard the dog moan when it hurt its leg.*

**sense** (sens) have meaning; be understandable
*He tried to make sense of his math work.*

**worth** (werth) good or important enough for
*That book is worth reading.*

# Will the Real King Please Stand Up?

***Necessary Words***

**horrible** (hôr´ ə bl) very bad; ugly; unpleasant

*It was horrible to see the boy get hit by the speeding car.*

# Will the Real King Please Stand Up?

*"There he is . . . kill him!" shouted the king. "It was Fouquet who had me put here!"*

***Preview:***

1. Read the name of the story.
2. Look at the picture.
3. Read the sentences under the picture.
4. Read the first paragraph of the story.
5. Then answer the following question.

You learned from your preview that Mr. Fouquet rode to the Bastille by

___ a. car.
___ b. train.
___ c. horse.
___ d. truck.

*Turn to the Comprehension Check on page 52 for the right answer.*

***Now read the story.***

Read to find out what happens to Philippe when Louis is set free.

# Will the Real King Please Stand Up?

Mr. Fouquet rode to the Bastille as fast as his horse could run. On the way there, all he could think about was the king. He did not understand how Aramis could do such a horrible thing. He only hoped that the king did not think that this whole thing was his fault.

As he entered the Bastille, he began calling for Baisemeaux.

"Who is there?" answered Baisemeaux.

"It is I, Fouquet. I want you to let the prisoner go, now!"

Poor Baisemeaux could not make sense of what had been going on during the past few days.

He said, "Which one? I hope you have a signed order from the king."

"As soon as you take me to the prisoner, I'll give you a signed order," replied Fouquet.

Baisemeaux called to a prison guard and said, "I wash my hands of this whole matter. Take Mr. Fouquet to the prisoner he wants."

As Fouquet walked away with the guard, Baisemeaux thought he had better stay away from D'Artagnan and his friends. The trouble they made was not worth it.

As he got closer to the prisoner, Fouquet heard a terrible moan.

"What is that sound?" he asked.

"That's the prisoner Aramis brought here last night," replied the guard.

"There he is, kill him! It was Fouquet who had me put here!" shouted the king.

The guard opened the door and Fouquet slowly walked to the king.

"Have you come to kill me now?" said the king.

"Oh, no, sir. I've come to free you," replied Fouquet.

"Why? It's your fault that I'm in here now," said the king.

"No sir, it is not. I know you were at my home, and it seems like it's my fault, but it is not. I came to free you as soon as Aramis told me the story," answered Fouquet.

"What does Aramis have to do with this?" asked the king.

Fouquet told him everything he knew.

"We must get rid of this man who pretends to be the king," said Louis.

As they left the Bastille, Fouquet gave a piece of paper to Baisemeaux.

Baisemeaux looked at the paper. It was an order signed by the king to set the prisoner free. Baisemeaux didn't know how Fouquet had gotten the order signed. What had gone on during Fouquet's short visit here? Baisemeaux decided that he needed more sleep and went back to bed.

At Fouquet's house, Philippe was in his room talking to his mother and D'Artagnan. He didn't know where Aramis was. He wished he would get back. Philippe felt bad because his mother didn't know who he was. She thought he was King Louis, just like everyone else. Just then the door opened and in walked Fouquet and Louis.

Philippe felt his heart beat. He did not know what to do.

Louis walked straight up to his mother and said, "My mother, do you know who I am?"

Then Philippe walked up to her and said the same thing.

The mother of the two kings just gave a soft moan and sat down. She felt bad about what she had done. She wondered if it had been worth it.

Louis went to D'Artagnan and looked him in the eye. He said, pointing to Philippe, "Have this man locked up. I want his face to be covered with an iron mask for the rest of his life."

D'Artagnan knew this was the real king talking because he seemed used to giving orders. He looked at Philippe and said, "I'm sorry. You are now my prisoner."

As D'Artagnan turned to leave the room, Fouquet said in a soft voice, "I think Aramis was right. This man is as much a king as Louis."

"No," said D'Artagnan. He is more of a king."

Then D'Artagnan took Philippe to the prison that would be his new home for the rest of his life. He would never be able to take the iron mask off.

Only now could D'Artagnan make sense of all that Aramis had been up to during the past few days.

# Will the Real King Please Stand Up?

## COMPREHENSION CHECK

**Preview Answer:**

c. horse.

***Choose the best answer.***

1. Mr. Fouquet was worried that
   ___a. Baisemeaux would not let the king out of prison.
   ___b. Aramis would catch up with him and stop him.
   ___c. Philippe was really not the twin brother of King Louis.
   ___d. King Louis would think that his problems were Mr. Fouquet's fault.

2. Baisemeaux
   ___a. was glad to see the real king set free.
   ___b. could not understand anything that had happened.
   ___c. called for D'Artagnan to help him find Philippe.
   ___d. went to the palace with Mr. Fouquet.

3. At first, King Louis
   ___a. was very happy to see Mr. Fouquet at the prison.
   ___b. told the guard to let Mr. Fouquet in to see him.
   ___c. blamed Mr. Fouquet for putting him in the Bastille.
   ___d. said it was all Baisemeaux's fault that he was in jail.

4. As Philippe was talking to his mother and D'Artagnan,
   ___a. Louis walked into the room.
   ___b. Aramis came to take him away.
   ___c. his mother knew who he really was by the way he spoke.
   ___d. D'Artagnan figured out that Philippe was not the king.

5. The queen
   ___a. was angry at Philippe for coming back.
   ___b. was glad that Philippe would never return.
   ___c. was afraid of what Louis would do to D'Artagnan.
   ___d. was surprised and saddened at all that had happened.

6. D'Artagnan
   ___a. was pleased that Philippe would be going to the Bastille.
   ___b. wanted to stay at the Bastille with Baisemeaux.
   ___c. did not like the way King Louis acted toward his brother.
   ___d. was happy to see King Louis come back.

7. At the end of the story, Mr. Fouquet
   ___a. was glad he had gone to the Bastille to get the king.
   ___b. knew he had made a mistake by freeing King Louis.
   ___c. said some very unkind things about Aramis.
   ___d. would not speak to D'Artagnan any more.

8. King Louis ordered D'Artagnan to put an iron mask on Philippe
   ___a. so that no one would ever be able to see that Philippe was his twin brother.
   ___b. because he thought that it would help Philippe.
   ___c. so that he could fight with Philippe using swords.
   ___d. because they were going to a costume party at Mr. Fouquet's palace.

9. Another name for this story could be
   ___a. "Aramis Wins."
   ___b. "Baisemeaux Returns."
   ___c. "Two Kings."
   ___d. "Philippe's Mother."

10. This story is mainly about
   ___a. what D'Artagnan does to help his friend Aramis save Philippe.
   ___b. how King Louis is freed from the Bastille to meet his brother Philippe.
   ___c. those people who try to keep Philippe from meeting his mother.
   ___d. where Aramis goes to hide from King Louis and his men.

*Check your answers with the key on page 67.*

# Will the Real King Please Stand Up?

## VOCABULARY CHECK

| during | fault | iron | moan | sense | worth |
|---|---|---|---|---|---|

### I. Sentences to Finish

***Fill in the blank in each sentence with the correct key word from the box above.***

1. Jason said it was his ________________ that the family was late for the show.
2. The show of colorful paintings is ________________ seeing.
3. I heard my brother ________________ when he dropped the book on his toe.
4. The tall fence and wide gates were made of ________________ .
5. We ate a large cup of popcorn ________________ the show.
6. Joe's idea to look for a car before he had the money, made no ________________ at all.

### II. Making Sense of Sentences

***Are the following sentences true or false? Place an X next to the correct answer.***

1. Something made out of <u>iron</u> would be made out of a hard metal. ____ True ____ False
2. A <u>moan</u> is a happy sound. ____ True ____ False
3. If an idea makes <u>sense</u>, it is understandable and has meaning. ____ True ____ False
4. If someone is at <u>fault</u>, they have made a mistake. ____ True ____ False
5. Something that happens <u>during</u> school, happens before or after you get there. ____ True ____ False
6. If a book is <u>worth</u> reading, it is not very important. ____ True ____ False

*Check your answers with the key on page 71.*

CTR C-49

# The King Gets Back at Aramis

## PREPARATION

### Key Words

| | | |
|---|---|---|
| **beach** | (bēch) | the part of the seashore over which water washes when high<br>*We played ball on the beach before we went swimming.* |
| **harbor** | (här´ bər) | a place of deep water with land on three sides where boats are sometimes kept<br>*We went to the harbor to watch the boats come in.* |
| **possible** | (pos´ ə bəl) | that can be done; that can happen<br>*Come to my house if possible.* |
| **speak** | (spēk) | say words; talk<br>*Please speak in a louder voice.* |
| **toward** | (tôrd) | turned to; facing<br>*He sat with his face toward the door.* |
| **trust** | (trust) | to believe in the truthfulness of someone or something<br>*I trust my good friend.* |

# *The King Gets Back at Aramis*

***Necessary Words***

**agree** (ə grē´) to have the same feeling as
*We agree on what to eat for dinner.*

**meanwhile** (mēn´ hwīl´) time between
*In the meanwhile, let's read.*

**meeting** (mē´ ting) a coming together
*We have a meeting at Cara's house next week.*

**quit** (kwit) stop; go away from; leave; give up
*He quit working at the store because he got a new job.*

**sail** (sāl) to travel on water by boat
*We went for a sail to the other side of the lake.*

**surround** (sə round´) shut in on all sides
*We will surround our yard with a fence.*

CTR C-49

# The King Gets Back at Aramis

*As D'Artagnan sails back to France, he hears the army open fire on Belle-Isle.*

**Preview:**

1. Read the name of the story.
2. Look at the picture.
3. Read the sentence under the picture.
4. Read the first four paragraphs of the story.
5. Then answer the following question.

You learned from your preview that D'Artagnan

___ a. wanted to kill Aramis and Porthos.
___ b. wanted to kill King Louis XIV.
___ c. wanted to help his friends escape.
___ d. wanted to help Philippe escape.

*Turn to the Comprehension Check on page 58 for the right answer.*

***Now read the story.***

Read to find out what the king had in store for D'Artagnan and his friends.

# *The King Gets Back at Aramis*

D'Artagnan had Philippe locked up for good. He then returned to the king. Louis told him that he now must go and kill Aramis and Porthos on Belle-Isle. The king knew that they were D'Artagnan's best friends.

"Will it be possible for you to kill your friends?" asked the king.

"Sir, your orders are all that matter. I shall take only the best guards with me," he replied.

D'Artagnan knew the king was right. How could he ever hurt his dear friends? He decided he would try to think of a plan to help his friends escape.

Meanwhile, Aramis and Porthos were wondering why the fishing boats had not returned for two days. Aramis felt something was wrong. As they stood on the beach and looked out to sea, they saw a boat. Then they saw another and another until the whole island was surrounded. Aramis then knew an escape was impossible. Soon they saw a small boat coming toward them. The man in the boat told them to come with him. They said they would not go unless they saw D'Artagnan first.

Soon D'Artagnan came back with the man. The young man would not let him speak to his friends. He had an order from the king that said not to leave D'Artagnan alone with his friends. D'Artagnan held his sword to the man's neck. The man then agreed to let the three friends speak.

Back on board his boat, D'Artagnan called all his men together. He explained what they must do to attack the harbor and kill the two men.

Once again, the young man had another signed order from the king. It said that D'Artagnan was ordered not to hold any meetings with his men until the island was taken and the two men killed.

"It seems the king no longer trusts me, so I must go and quit my job as head musketeer! Turn the boat around. I shall go see the king at once!" spoke D'Artagnan.

Once more the young man pulled out an order from the king. It said that as soon as D'Artagnan tried to quit his job, he was no longer in charge. The young man would now give the orders. D'Artagnan must return to France.

D'Artagnan knew he had lost. He turned to the man and said, "I shall leave now."

One last time he looked toward the harbor and saw his two friends on the beach. He thought maybe when he got back to France he could speak to the king and change things. It did not seem like it was possible, but he could try. After all, these were his best friends.

Back on the island, Porthos and Aramis began to plan their escape. They were not worried. They had complete trust in their friend D'Artagnan. They knew he would not harm them. What they did not know was that D'Artagnan's plan had not worked and he was on his way back to France. They would have to escape alone.

As D'Artagnan sailed back to France, he heard the army open fire on Belle-Isle. As the guns kept firing, D'Artagnan kept hoping the attack would not work and his friends would escape.

# The King Gets Back at Aramis

## COMPREHENSION CHECK

**Preview Answer:**

c. wanted to help his friends escape.

***Choose the best answer.***

1. Philippe
   ___a. escaped from the Bastille.
   ___b. went to live with his mother, the queen.
   ___c. stayed at Mr. Fouquet's palace.
   ___d. was locked up in the Bastille forever.

2. In the beginning of the story, D'Artagnan
   ___a. knew he had to find Aramis and Porthos and follow the king's orders.
   ___b. tried to get the king's men to turn against the king.
   ___c. pretended that he would find and kill his friends Aramis and Porthos.
   ___d. had already saved Philippe from the Bastille and had taken him away.

3. As Aramis and Porthos waited for the fishing boats to return, Belle-Isle was
   ___a. covered with thick clouds.
   ___b. slowly surrounded by boats.
   ___c. flooded by a heavy rain.
   ___d. burned by the king's men.

4. Aramis and Porthos
   ___a. would not go with the man on the boat until they saw D'Artagnan.
   ___b. went to find a different island on which to hide.
   ___c. went back to France with the man on the boat to see King Louis.
   ___d. would not speak to D'Artagnan because he took Philippe.

5. King Louis
   ___a. did not trust D'Artagnan to kill his friends.
   ___b. gave an order to kill D'Artagnan no matter what happened.
   ___c. trusted D'Artagnan more than anyone else.
   ___d. came to Belle-Isle to find Aramis and Porthos himself.

6. First, D'Artagnan tried to quit his job as musketeer. Then, a young man took his place by order of the king. Next,
   ___a. D'Artagnan fired on the island.
   ___b. D'Artagnan saved Aramis and Porthos in his boat.
   ___c. D'Artagnan had to return to France.
   ___d. D'Artagnan jumped into the water and swam to the harbor.

7. Aramis and Porthos
   ___a. knew they had to escape without help from D'Artagnan.
   ___b. did not know that D'Artagnan's plan had failed.
   ___c. understood that they would never see D'Artagnan again.
   ___d. were waiting on the island to speak to King Louis.

8. At the end of the story,
   ___a. D'Artagnan was killed by the army.
   ___b. Aramis and Porthos were off the island.
   ___c. the army attacked the island of Belle-Isle.
   ___d. the young man in charge gave up and sailed away.

9. Another name for this story could be
   ___a. "D'Artagnan Wins the Fight."
   ___b. "The Sinking of D'Artagnan's Ship."
   ___c. "The King Forgives Aramis."
   ___d. "Trouble on Belle-Isle."

10. This story is mainly about
   ___a. the people who live on the island of Belle-Isle.
   ___b. how D'Artagnan tries to save his friends at Belle-Isle.
   ___c. why the king is going back to France.
   ___d. the fishing boats going off to sea.

*Check your answers with the key on page 67.*

# The King Gets Back at Aramis

## VOCABULARY CHECK

| beach | harbor | possible | speak | toward | trust |
|---|---|---|---|---|---|

### I. Sentences to Finish

***Fill in the blank in each sentence with the correct key word from the box above.***

1. We watched the sea gulls fly over the sand and water at the ________________ .
2. The teacher asked me to ________________ loudly and clearly so that the children in the back of the room could hear me.
3. There were many ships with tall sails at the ________________ .
4. I turned ________________ the west to watch the sun set.
5. It is ________________ that my sister will come home early today.
6. Sam would ________________ Zack with his best coins, stamps, and bottle tops.

### II. Matching

***Write the letter of the correct meaning from Column B next to the key word in Column A.***

| | Column A | | Column B |
|---|---|---|---|
| _____1. | beach | a. | a place with deep water with land on three sides where boats are kept |
| _____2. | harbor | b. | say words; talk |
| _____3. | possible | c. | to believe in the truthfulness of someone or something |
| _____4. | speak | d. | the part of the seashore over which water washes |
| _____5. | toward | e. | turned to; facing |
| _____6. | trust | f. | that can be done or that can happen |

*Check your answers with the key on page 71.*

# The End of the Musketeers

## *PREPARATION*

### *Key Words*

| | | |
|---|---|---|
| **barrel** | (bar´ əl) | something made of wood with a round, flat top and bottom, used for holding things<br>*We had a whole barrel full of apples.* |
| **die** | (dī) | to stop living<br>*If your heart stops beating, you will die.* |
| **receive** | (ri sēv´) | be given; to take into one's hands<br>*You will receive something nice for your birthday.* |
| **understood** | (un´ dər stůd´) | got the meaning of<br>*I understood what she said.* |
| **weak** | (wēk) | not strong<br>*Her arms felt weak from holding the big box.* |
| **won** | (wun) | not to have lost; to be the better of<br>*We won the game easily.* |

# The End of the Musketeers

***Necessary Words***

| | | |
|---|---|---|
| **boulder** | (bōl′ dər) | a very large rock<br>*We sat on the boulder by the lake.* |
| **lit** | (lit) | to have started something burning<br>*We lit a fire in the fireplace.* |
| **forgive** | (fər giv′) | not have hard feelings toward<br>*I forgive you for taking my book.* |
| **fought** | (fôt) | a battle or disagreement<br>*We fought over who would have the best part in the play.* |

***Places***

**Spain** is a country in Europe, near France.

# The End of the Musketeers

*The rocks of the cave began to fall. Will Porthos be able to make it to safety?*

***Preview:***

1. Read the name of the story.
2. Look at the picture.
3. Read the sentences under the picture.
4. Read the first three paragraphs of the story.
5. Then answer the following question.

You learned from your preview that Aramis and Porthos were

___ a. ready to die.
___ b. feeling very weak.
___ c. going to kill a wild pig.
___ d. ready to make their escape.

*Turn to the Comprehension Check on page 64 for the right answer.*

***Now read the story.***

Read to find out what happens to Aramis and Porthos.

# The End of the Musketeers

After D'Artagnan left Belle-Isle, Aramis said, "It's time for us to make our escape. Soon we will be free. Why do you look so sad, Porthos?"

"Let me tell you something. The day my grandfather was killed by a wild pig, his legs felt weak. Then a few hours before my own father was to die, he told my mother his legs were weak. Right now my own legs feel weak," replied Porthos.

"Well, my friend, just because that happened twice, does not mean it will happen a third time," said Aramis.

"I guess," agreed Porthos, "but let's make our get-away now!"

The people of Belle-Isle were now friends with the two men. They had told them about some caves that went out to the sea. The two friends planned to leave the island through the caves.

Just then they heard screaming. The king's guards were attacking the people of Belle-Isle. Porthos and Aramis began fighting the guards. The people of Belle-Isle joined them. Aramis knew they would never win this fight. He told the good people of Belle-Isle that the guards had won. They must give up so they wouldn't be killed.

Aramis took Porthos to the caves. He said, "Let's try to make our escape now. The guards are busy and the people are safe. Let's go!"

Porthos followed closely behind Aramis. He tripped a few times. His legs were getting weaker.

There were two men at the caves waiting to help them make their escape. As they entered the caves, they heard noise behind them. The guards were close behind, and they had hunting dogs with them. It was the first time the two men really understood that they might die.

The men who were helping them escape had made ready a big barrel full of gunpowder. Aramis asked Porthos if he was strong enough to throw it. Porthos said, "Light it."

Aramis lit the barrel and he and the two men ran. Porthos threw the barrel and turned to run. Just then, his legs gave out again. He couldn't move. He was so close to the way out of the cave that he could see Aramis waiting for him in the boat. Porthos could escape if only he could move. The barrel went off and the king's guards all ran the other way. Porthos finally stood up, but it was too late. The rocks of the cave began to fall on him. He held up a great boulder for a while but he just wasn't strong enough. Porthos went down and the boulder covered him. Aramis understood that his dear friend had died.

Back in France, the king had forgiven D'Artagnan. He told him that he understood how he felt about his friends. He told him that Porthos had died and that Aramis had finally escaped. He was now living in Spain.

Since D'Artagnan had worked for the king many years, he agreed to keep working for Louis.

Twelve years later, Aramis met D'Artagnan again. D'Artagnan told him how Athos had died. Aramis told his old friend about the last time he and Porthos had been on Belle-Isle.

They were now only two musketeers. The two friends said good-by to each other. They didn't think they would ever see each other again.

Shortly after, D'Artagnan went to fight for the king. He fought very hard. He won many fights. The last one was just too much for him. As he lay on the ground, about to die, one of the guards brought him a note from the king. He was to receive the highest medal in France for his great work. He died a happy man because he had always wanted to receive that medal.

The days of the four musketeers were now over, for only Aramis still lived.

As for Philippe, he lived the rest of his life in prison, his face covered with an iron mask.

# The End of the Musketeers

## COMPREHENSION CHECK

**Preview Answer:**

d. ready to make their escape.

***Choose the best answer.***

1. Porthos believed his legs felt weak because
   ___a. he had not eaten anything for a long time.
   ___b. he was going to die soon.
   ___c. he had become ill, suddenly.
   ___d. he hurt his feet running through the woods.

2. The people of Belle-Isle
   ___a. did not like Porthos and Aramis.
   ___b. tried to catch Porthos and Aramis.
   ___c. told the king's men where to find Porthos and Aramis.
   ___d. helped Porthos and Aramis in their escape.

3. The guards
   ___a. went back to France.
   ___b. stayed in their boats at sea.
   ___c. came onto the island to attack the people.
   ___d. left their dogs on the island and went home.

4. The best way for Porthos and Aramis to escape
   ___a. was through the caves.
   ___b. was in a small box they found.
   ___c. was through two large gates.
   ___d. was on a large fishing boat.

5. First, Aramis lit the barrel of gunpowder and ran. Then, Porthos threw the barrel. Next,
   ___a. the barrel did not explode.
   ___b. Porthos's legs became too weak for him to leave the cave.
   ___c. the dogs came up to Porthos and tried to bite him.
   ___d. the king's men captured Aramis.

6. When the barrel went off,
   ___a. the king's men kept coming toward Porthos.
   ___b. Aramis was still in the cave.
   ___c. the rocks in the cave began to fall on Porthos.
   ___d. Porthos was in the boat with Aramis.

7. Many years after Belle-Isle, D'Artagnan
   ___a. died in a battle for King Louis and received a medal.
   ___b. lived in Spain with his friend Aramis.
   ___c. still would not work for King Louis.
   ___d. returned to France to see Philippe become king.

8. At the end of the story, the only musketeer who was still alive was
   ___a. Porthos.
   ___b. D'Artagnan.
   ___c. Athos.
   ___d. Aramis.

9. Another name for this story could be
   ___a. "Friends to the End."
   ___b. "A Storm at Sea."
   ___c. "Aramis Joins the Guards."
   ___d. "A Fire on Belle-Isle."

10. This story is mainly about
   ___a. how King Louis was killed in a great battle.
   ___b. what finally happened to the musketeers.
   ___c. what happened to Porthos's father and grandfather.
   ___d. how the people left the island of Belle-Isle.

*Check your answers with the key on page 67.*

# The End of the Musketeers

## VOCABULARY CHECK

| barrel | die | receive | understood | weak | won |
|---|---|---|---|---|---|

### I. Sentences to Finish

***Fill in the blank in each sentence with the correct key word from the box above.***

1. Every month I __________________ a new book in the mail.
2. Angelina worked as hard as she could and __________________ the contest.
3. In the autumn the maple leaves change color, fall from the trees, and __________________ .
4. We picked apples from the trees and put them in a big __________________ .
5. I feel __________________ if I don't eat enough food.
6. Mark __________________ the story after he read it again.

### II. Mixed-up Words

***First, unscramble the letters in Column A to spell out the key words. Then, match the key words with the right meaning in Column B by drawing a line from the word to its meaning.***

| Column A | Column B |
|---|---|
| 1. eid ____________________________ | a. got the meaning of |
| 2. odtsoudnre ______________________ | b. not strong |
| 3. keaw ___________________________ | c. to stop living |
| 4. ciervee _________________________ | d. something made of wood with a round, flat top and bottom, used for holding things |
| 5. lerbar __________________________ | e. be given |
| 6. onw ____________________________ | f. not to have lost |

*Check your answers with the key on page 72.*

# NOTES

# COMPREHENSION CHECK ANSWER KEY
## Lessons CTR C-41 to CTR C-50

| LESSON NUMBER | QUESTION NUMBER | | | | | | | | | | PAGE NUMBER |
|---|---|---|---|---|---|---|---|---|---|---|---|
| | 1 | 2 | 3 | 4 | 5 | 6 | 7 | 8 | 9 | 10 | |
| CTR C-41 | c | b | c | d | c | d | ○a | ○b | △b | □c | 10 |
| CTR C-42 | b | d | c | d | ○b | ○c | a | c | △b | □c | 16 |
| CTR C-43 | c | a | d | ○b | ○d | ◇b | ○a | c | △d | □c | 22 |
| CTR C-44 | c | d | b | d | a | c | a | ○d | △b | □c | 28 |
| CTR C-45 | b | ○c | a | d | b | d | c | a | △d | □b | 34 |
| CTR C-46 | ○b | c | ○a | d | ○c | b | a | d | △b | □d | 40 |
| CTR C-47 | ○b | ○d | ○c | ○a | d | b | c | ◇a | △b | □c | 46 |
| CTR C-48 | d | b | c | a | d | ○c | ○b | a | △c | □b | 52 |
| CTR C-49 | d | c | b | a | ○a | ◇c | b | c | △d | □b | 58 |
| CTR C-50 | ○b | d | c | a | ◇b | c | a | d | △a | □b | 64 |

◇ = **Sequence**

○ = **Inference**

△ = **Another name for the story**

□ = **Main idea of the story**

# NOTES

# VOCABULARY CHECK ANSWER KEY

## Lessons CTR C-41 to CTR C-50

| LESSON NUMBER | | PAGE NUMBER |
|---|---|---|
| **41** | **A VERY STRANGE DINNER** | **11** |

*I.*
1. free
2. sir
3. palace
4. adventure
5. charge
6. order

*II.*

| | | | | | | | | |
|---|---|---|---|---|---|---|---|---|
| H | E | T | O | N | E | M | V | U |
| P | I | H | S | R | M | W | O | D |
| A | D | V | E | N | T | U | R | E |
| L | G | I | T | S | F | U | D | B |
| A | X | J | O | N | R | M | E | V |
| C | H | A | R | G | E | L | R | S |
| E | Z | K | O | B | E | S | I | R |
| B | P | A | L | A | C | E | T | K |

| | | |
|---|---|---|
| **42** | **THE SECRET PRISONER** | **17** |

*I.*
1. nod
2. queen
3. shine
4. interest
5. spoke
6. guard

*II.*
1. True
2. True
3. True
4. True
5. False
6. True

| | | |
|---|---|---|
| **43** | **PHILIPPE TELLS HIS STORY** | **23** |

*I.*
1. spend
2. prove
3. imagine
4. truth
5. also
6. parent

*II.*

| | | | | | | | | | | |
|---|---|---|---|---|---|---|---|---|---|---|
| | | | | | | | | | | 4 S |
| | | | | | | | | | | P |
| | | | | | | 3 P | R | O | V | E |
| | | | | | | A | | | | N |
| | | | | | | R | | | | D |
| 1 I | M | 2 A | G | I | N | E | | | | |
| | | L | | | | N | | | | |
| | | S | | | | 5 T | R | U | T | H |
| | | O | | | | | | | | |

# VOCABULARY CHECK ANSWER KEY

## Lessons CTR C-41 to CTR C-50

**LESSON NUMBER** | **PAGE NUMBER**

**44 A VISIT TO THE KING'S TAILOR** **29**

*I.* 1. center
2. complete
3. having
4. sigh
5. giant
6. cheer

*II.* 1. c
2. d
3. f
4. b
5. e
6. a

**45 ANOTHER DINNER AT THE BASTILLE** **35**

*I.* 1. delicious
2. reason
3. captain
4. plan
5. dine
6. dare

*II.*

| | | | | | | | | | | | |
|---|---|---|---|---|---|---|---|---|---|---|---|
| | | | | | | | | | | | 2 R |
| | | | | | | | | | | | E |
| | | | | | | | | | | | A |
| | | | 1 D | E | L | I | 4 C | I | O | U | S |
| | | | A | | | | A | | | | O |
| | | | R | | | | P | | | | N |
| 3 D | I | N | E | | | | T | | | | |
| | | | | | | | A | | | | |
| | | | | | | | I | | | | |
| | | | | 5 P | L | A | N | | | | |

**46 THE SWITCH** **41**

*I.* 1. whole
2. act
3. explain
4. wake
5. exactly
6. main

*II.* 1. whole, f
2. main, d
3. exactly, e
4. wake, a
5. act, c
6. explain, b

# VOCABULARY CHECK ANSWER KEY

## Lessons CTR C-41 to CTR C-50

| LESSON NUMBER | | PAGE NUMBER |
|---|---|---|
| 47 | THE STORY IS TOLD | 47 |

*I.*
1. enter
2. handle
3. heart
4. chest
5. hour
6. hammer

*II.*

| | | | | | | | |
|---|---|---|---|---|---|---|---|
| O | L | D | P | I | K | Z | V |
| C | I | H | A | M | M | E | R |
| H | N | A | B | S | O | N | E |
| E | Z | N | E | H | X | T | P |
| S | K | D | C | O | B | E | X |
| T | A | L | M | U | Y | R | I |
| O | H | E | A | R | T | B | U |
| M | K | O | L | C | V | E | W |

**48 WILL THE REAL KING PLEASE STAND UP?** 53

*I.*
1. fault
2. worth
3. moan
4. iron
5. during
6. sense

*II.*
1. True
2. False
3. True
4. True
5. False
6. False

**49 THE KING GETS BACK AT ARAMIS** 59

*I.*
1. beach
2. speak
3. harbor
4. toward
5. possible
6. trust

*II.*
1. d
2. a
3. f
4. b
5. e
6. c

# VOCABULARY CHECK ANSWER KEY

## Lessons CTR C-41 to CTR C-50

| LESSON NUMBER | | PAGE NUMBER |
|---|---|---|
| 50 | THE END OF THE MUSKETEERS | 65 |

*I.*
1. receive
2. won
3. die
4. barrel
5. weak
6. understood

*II.*
1. die, c
2. understood, a
3. weak, b
4. receive, e
5. barrel, d
6. won, f